SNAKES

SEYMOUR SIMON

Smithsonian | Collins

An Imprint of HarperCollins*Publishers*

PICTURE CREDITS
pp. 6, 10, 15, 17, 25, 31, 32 © Jim Bridges; pp. 4, 9, 18 © K. H. Switak; pp. 13, 21, 23, 26 © J. Cancalosi; p. 29 © Alan Carey.
page 32: Florida kingsnake eggs hatching
The name of the Smithsonian, Smithsonian Institution and the sunburst logo
are registered trademarks of the Smithsonian Institution.
Collins is an imprint of HarperCollins Publishers.

Snakes
Library of Congress Cataloging-in-Publication Data
Simon, Seymour.
Snakes / by Seymour Simon.
p. cm.
Summary: Describes, in text and photographs, the physical characteristics, habits, and natural environment
of various species of snakes.
ISBN-10: 0-06-114096-1 (trade bdg.) — ISBN-13: 978-0-06-114096-9 (trade bdg.)
ISBN-10: 0-06-114095-3 (pbk.) — ISBN-13: 978-0-06-114095-2 (pbk.)
1. Snakes—Juvenile literature. [1. Snakes.] I. Title.
QL666.O6S456 1992   91-15948
597.96—dc20   CIP
                                                                                                              AC
1 2 3 4 5 6 7 8 9 10
❖
Revised Edition

Smithsonian Mission Statement

For more than 160 years, the Smithsonian has remained true to its mission, "the increase and diffusion of knowledge." Today the Smithsonian is not only the world's largest provider of museum experiences supported by authoritative scholarship in science, history, and the arts but also an international leader in scientific research and exploration. The Smithsonian offers the world a picture of America, and America a picture of the world.

There are about twenty-nine hundred different kinds of snakes in the world. Some people think all snakes are venomous. But in fact, only a few hundred kinds are venomous, and only about fifty of these are really dangerous to humans. Most snakes are harmless. Snakes stay away from people as much as they can.

Snakes live all over the world except for the Arctic and Antarctic, Iceland, Ireland, New Zealand, and some small oceanic islands. Most snakes live on or under the ground; some live in trees, and a few others spend all or part of their lives in water. Snakes, such as this emerald tree boa, are often colorful, with a variety of beautiful patterns on their skins. Many behave in odd and unusual ways. Snakes are among the most interesting creatures on earth.

Snakes are reptiles and are related to lizards, turtles, alligators, and crocodiles. Like other reptiles, snakes have backbones and scaly skins, and are cold-blooded. That does not mean that they are cold, but that the temperature of a snake's body depends upon the temperature around it. Snakes need warm surroundings to be active. For this reason, most snakes are found in warm regions or are active mainly during the warm weather.

Most snakes do not have legs, and their **cylinder**-shaped body may be as short as your finger or as long as a school bus. A snake is not just a head attached to a long tail. Its tail starts after the opening of the **cloaca** on the underside of its body, and can be anywhere from a few inches to a third of its body length. The rest of a snake's body contains its heart, lungs, stomach, and other organs.

Humans have thirty-three small bones, called **vertebrae**, that make up their backbones. But some long snakes have as many as five hundred vertebrae. Because of its many vertebrae, a snake, such as this rear-fanged island vine snake, can easily bend its body this way and that.

A snake is strong for its size. Pound for pound, snakes are among the strongest of animals.

Snakes can't walk or run, but they have four ways of moving. The most common is called serpentine **locomotion**. The snake contracts its muscles to produce a series of loops in its body. As each loop pushes backward against the surface, the snake moves forward. Snakes can move quickly this way along the ground or on a tree branch, but most snakes can be easily outdistanced by a running person.

Concertina locomotion (named after an accordion) is used by some burrowing snakes. The snake coils itself together and extends the front end of its body forward. Then the snake anchors its front end and pulls its back end forward. In caterpillar locomotion, snakes with thick bodies, such as boas, grip the ground with their enlarged belly scales to move forward.

Still another kind of snake motion is called sidewinding. Some kinds of rattlesnakes and vipers use sidewinding to move across loose desert sand. A sidewinder loops its body off the ground and moves in a pattern similar to serpentine locomotion, except that two or three sections of its body are off the ground at one time. The tracks of a sidewinder look like the rungs of a crooked ladder.

Snakes can also climb trees and swim.

Some snakes grow their entire lives. They grow much more quickly when they are young. Rattlesnakes may double in length by the end of the first year, and some pythons may even triple in length during that time. A ball python, shown here, usually grows a foot a year for its first three years. The rate of growth depends upon the kind of snake, the available food, the climate, and the individual. The rate of growth slows as snakes age but may never stop completely as it does with humans and other mammals. An old snake will grow only a little bit, but it may still grow.

It is difficult to know how long snakes live in the wild. But some kinds of snakes have lived in zoos for more than twenty years.

All snakes eat animals. Either they lie quietly and blend into their surrounding until the **prey** comes close enough to be struck, or else they sneak up on it. Many snakes eat animals that humans consider pests, like rats and mice. No snake chews it prey. The snake can open its jaws wide enough to swallow a whole animal that may be much larger than the snake's head.

Almost any animal that is not too big can be a meal for a snake. Small snakes, such as this yellow ratsnake, can eat insects, lizards, birds and their eggs, fish, and rodents. Larger snakes can also feed on rabbits, deer, monkeys, pigs, chickens, sheep, and goats. It may take a large snake hours to swallow a really big animal such as a pig or a goat, and it may be weeks or even months before the snake needs another meal. The time depends upon the size and the shape of the prey.

Snakes use senses such as touch to help them find their prey and avoid danger. But their senses of sight, hearing, and smell are different from ours. Snakes do not see color. They see shades of gray. They do not see shapes as humans do, but they can still spot the slightest movement around them.

Snakes have internal ears, which means their ears are not on the outside of their bodies. Snakes do not hear the full range of sounds that travel through the air. But they can easily feel ground vibrations—even the quiet rustling of an approaching mouse.

Snakes also have an excellent sense of smell. A snake's forked tongue picks up tiny particles of prey odors that float in the air or on the ground. Then the tongue carries the particles back to two small odor-sensing pits, called Jacobson's organs, in the roof of the mouth. Some snakes, such as this copperhead, have heat-sensing pits in front of their eyes so that they can track warm animals even at night.

Snakes are not slimy. A snake's skin is hard and smooth to allow the snake to slide easily over the ground. Its scales are thickened, hardened parts of the outer layers of skin. Snakes' eyes are covered by thin, transparent scales called spectacles. A snake's skin is important to its survival. The colors and patterns of the skin may help to hide the snake among its surroundings, or they may serve to warn enemies away.

Snakes have two layers of skin, the epidermis, or outer layer, and the dermis. As the snake grows larger, it sheds its thin outer skin, including the eye spectacles, to make room for its growing body. Before it sheds the old skin, the snake grows a new outer skin. Young, quickly growing snakes may shed six or more times a year. Body scales can be strangely shaped, like the "horns" on the head of this eyelash viper.

Many **temperate-zone** snakes mate in the spring. Female snakes usually lay eggs in the early summer. Egg-laying snakes are called oviparous [oh-VIP-uh-rus]. Egg-laying species include pythons, hognoses, coralsnakes, milk snakes, and kingsnakes.

Snakes lay their eggs in damp rotting wood, in holes in the ground, or in deserted animal burrows. This green tree python's eggs are long and narrow and protected by a tough, leathery covering. While python mothers coil about their eggs and remain with them for two months or longer until they hatch, kingsnake eggs are left to hatch on their own, warmed by the sun. Untended snake eggs take between six to eight weeks to hatch. A baby snake has an egg tooth to help it cut through the shell. The quicker the eggs hatch the better. Unhatched eggs may be eaten by animals that chance upon them.

Garter snakes, boas, watersnakes, and pitvipers keep their developing **embryos** within their own bodies until the embryos develop fully. Then they bear living young. Live-bearing snakes are called viviparous [vy-VIP-uh-rus]. Most young snakes live on their own and are not taken care of by their mothers.

Snakes have many enemies waiting to snap them up for a meal. Baby snakes are killed and eaten by frogs, pigs, skunks, hedgehogs, opossums, badgers, foxes, coyotes, and many other animals. Some animals, such as mongooses, have the quickness to bite and kill even venomous cobras. Birds such as eagles and hawks regularly prey upon snakes. An eagle or a hawk will plunge down from the sky and grip a snake with its claws before the snake can defend itself. The bird then kills the snake with its sharp beak. Long-legged birds such as secretary birds and road runners regularly hunt and kill snakes.

Some snakes, such as kingsnakes and racers, regularly feed upon smaller snakes. This king male is swallowing a young rattlesnake. Humans are probably the biggest threat to snakes, because they destroy the wild places that snakes need to live. Some people will unreasonably kill any kind of snake, even if it is harmless and poses no danger.

About three quarters of all snakes are generally harmless and belong to a family called Colubridae. Among the colubrids are garter snakes, watersnakes, ratsnakes, grass snakes, milk snakes, and racers. None of these is very large, none has front fangs, and each has a different way of protecting itself. Some have skin colors and patterns that blend in with their surroundings. Other kinds of snakes hiss at an enemy or rear up in a threatening way. Some also flatten their bodies, which makes them look larger and more dangerous than they really are.

The most unusual defensive behavior among these harmless snakes is that of the hognoses. These snakes get their name from their upturned snout, which is used for digging in the ground. When you startle a hognose, it puffs out its head and body and sways back and forth like a miniature cobra. Come too close, and the hognose will hiss loudly and open its jaws wide. Hognoses are rear-fanged snakes. But the hognose seldom bites. If it is still being bothered after its fearsome display, the hognose will suddenly roll over on its back. It looks as if the snake is dead. But if you flip the hognose right side up, it will immediately flip over on its back again and remain that way until the danger has passed.

The biggest snakes are the longest land animals that are alive today—longer than an elephant or a giraffe. These giant snakes use their flexible bodies to throw coils around their prey. Scientists once believed that the prey dies of suffocation, or lack of air. New research has shown that the tightening coils slowly squeeze the chest cavity of the prey, causing the heart to stop beating.

Giant snakes rarely attack people. If one does, it is probably because the snake mistakes the person for an animal that it normally preys upon. A person is more likely to be hit by lightning than attacked by a giant snake.

All the giant snakes are either boas or pythons and belong to the Boidae or Pythonidae families. (Not all boas and pythons are giants; there are many smaller kinds.) If you take length, thickness, and heaviness into account, the anaconda (a boa) is the biggest snake in the world. There are reports of anacondas in the wild that measured over thirty feet long. (Some biologists argue that the reticulate python can be as long as an anaconda.) Anacondas live in swamps and on lake and river banks in tropical parts of South America, where this one was photographed.

Most venomous snakes in the United States belong to a family called Viperidae, or vipers. Vipers have large venom glands in their heads, connected by ducts to long, curved venom fangs in the front of the upper jaws. When not in use, the hinged fangs fold back and lie flat. When a viper is ready to bite, the fangs rotate forward and venom flows into them through the ducts.

The viper family is made up of two large subfamilies: true vipers and pitvipers. True vipers live mostly in Africa, with a few kinds in Europe and Asia. True vipers include the Gaboon viper, the puff adder, and the European adder, the only venomous snake in England.

Pitvipers, named for the heat-sensing pits on their heads, live in the Americas and Asia and include about twenty kinds of rattlesnakes, the water moccasin (or cottonmouth), and the copperhead. Rattlesnakes, such as this diamondback, live mainly in the southeastern and southwestern United States and northwest Mexico, but some rattlers are found in every other mainland state except Maine and Delaware. The rattle is made up of special interlocking scales at the end of the tail. When the tail is shaken, the rattles hit against each other and make a noise like a buzzing insect that often frightens away enemies.

Cobras, mambas, coralsnakes, taipans, and death adders belong to another family of venomous snakes, called Elapidae. Elapids are found mostly in Asia, Africa, Australia, and tropical America, though coralsnakes are found from Florida north to the Carolinas and west to Texas. Most elapids have fixed, hollow venom fangs that are always erect and ready for use.

The king cobra is the largest of all venomous snakes, sometimes reaching a length of more than fifteen feet. The Indian cobra, shown here, is also known as the spectacled cobra because of the eyelike markings on its hood. It raises its hood by spreading the ribs of its neck. Because the Indian cobra is commonly found in populated areas of India and southeast Asia, it is far more likely to bite a person than is the rarer king cobra.

Australia is the only continent with more venomous than nonvenomous kinds of snakes. Two of the most deadly are the death adder and the taipan. The death adder has hinged fangs, while the taipan has fixed fangs set in the front of its mouth. The bite of a death adder is often fatal. The taipan is a large snake that grows to more than ten feet. Taipans, like most snakes, avoid people. If threatened, taipans defend themselves with very rapid strikes. A person who is bitten by this snake and does not receive prompt medical treatment may die within a few hours.

In the United States on average there are between nine and fifteen deaths a year from snakebites. India has the highest number of fatal snakebites—between ten and twenty *thousand* deaths each year.

Of course, venomous snakes that come into houses or farms must be destroyed. But snakes, including venomous kinds, such as this golden eyelash viper, play an important role in nature by keeping down the rodent population that eats crops and carries disease. If all snakes were to disappear, rodents would increase greatly, crops would be destroyed, and there might be more human suffering because of lack of food or the spread of disease than snakes could ever cause.

To appreciate the special qualities of snakes is to appreciate the diversity and importance of all life in our world.

GLOSSARY

Cloaca—The cavity into which the intestinal, reproductive, and urinary canals empty.

Cylinder—An object with straight sides and circular ends, which is the general form of a snake's body.

Embryo—A developing animal in the early stages of growth before hatching or birth.

Locomotion—Movement from one point to another; can describe the motion of an animal.

Prey—An animal that is hunted or caught by another animal for food.

Temperate zone—Region between the Tropic of Capricorn and the Antarctic Circle or the region between the Tropic of Cancer and the Arctic Circle; these regions are defined by their moderate, or mild, climates.

Vertebrae—The series of bones forming the spinal column, or backbone; humans and other animals, such as snakes, have vertebrae.